The Linas

In Troy Missouri

By: John Lina

May 1, 2011

The Linas in Troy Missouri

Prolog

My Grandfather, Anton Lina, was born on September 16, 1879 and arrived in this country on October 24, 1905 from Weisskirchen (BelaCrkva) in what is now Serbia. It was part of the former Yugoslavia and before that part of the Austro-Hungarian Empire until it was split up after the First World War. I found an old map of the area and verified the name Weisskirchen plus it is listed as the birthplace of my Uncle John, my Grandparents' oldest son.

Grandpa

The Linas in Troy Missouri

Grandma

John (Uncle John) was born in February 1906; the year after Grandpa came over. Then Irma, my grandmother, arrived on October 9, 1906 and Edmond, my Dad, was born in October 1907. So it all works out chronologically. They had a third son, Anton (Uncle Tony) in June 1909 and that was the end of the baby making for the two of them.

The Linas in Troy Missouri

Eddie, Tony, John, Grandma

Eddie, Tony, and John with Grandma

The Linas in Troy Missouri

My Grandfather met a man on the ship who told him there were good jobs to be had in Saint Louis and that's where he went. I suppose he found work, saved some money, sent for Irma, and brought her and baby John to the USA. There is a picture of a young looking Anton in-group with other workers in a locomotive factory.

The Locomotive Factory Picture

Then my dad said he was a pin stripe painter for a carriage works, then for automobiles. I know for sure he was a painter because I know that he left

The Linas in Troy Missouri

Troy a couple of times to do some building painting in other locations not very far away. Plus the fact that he ended up with liver cancer which was/is an occupational hazard for anyone who works around lead, which was the main ingredient of white paint at the time.

My Grandmother was very young when she married in February of 1905, only 16, and my Grandfather was 26 there was a 10 year difference. They were born in September 1879 and April 1888. He died in July 1952 and she died in September 1956. My dad said the marriage was arranged by others. She came from a town named Resita in Romania but it's only about fifty-five miles from Bela Crkva and it would have been in the same country at that time.

They found a place to live in Saint Louis, near Salisbury and Blair; the house was on the alley at the back of the lot. Saint Louis had an incredibly high population density with a peak in 1930 of 856,960 people living in a city of 62 square miles or 21 people per acre; or one person for a square 45'on a side. When you deduct streets, parks,

The Linas in Troy Missouri

and commercial/industrial acreages; one can see that it was very dense. This would explain why every little bit of ground was used to build places for people to live. In 1900 it was 575,000 and in 1910 it was 687,000.

They must have lived here for a while because my dad and his brothers went to Clay Elementary School. At some point they moved to Davidson Avenue in Walnut Park and lived there until April 1932. It was during the depression, Grandpa was out of work. My dad said Grandma was feeling the social pressure of the situation. I'd heard that Grandpa was depressed by it. In any event times were hard.

Grandma was something of a social person in Saint Louis. There are pictures of her with her Austrian Women's Society. But it is not reasonable to think that she would up and move out to Troy Missouri because of some imagined stigma.

The Linas in Troy Missouri

The Motivation

How they found out about Troy Missouri and the place they bought is not known. In 1930, the whole of Lincoln County had a population of less than 14,000 on 630 square miles or 0.03 people per acre. The location is "out in the boon docks" to say the least and it was even further isolated then. And yet there is a thread of something in my memory that triggers a possibility.

It could well be that they were "sold" on the idea of chicken farming by an operator of a collection company. This is my own coined term for the reverse of a distribution company. It is a stretch of the imagination to think that they found South Troy on their own. It is easier to rationalize that they came across information, perhaps from an ad, about the income to be gained from the chicken and egg business, contacted the company, got referred to this place in the country, and took the deal. It may have been a way out of the situation they were in, which may have seemed dire.

The Linas in Troy Missouri

When they moved out there they went into the business. They had an operation that consisted of laying hens, fryers and pullets; they would collect eggs daily and keep them in crates in the house and a man would come by and pick them up. Periodically the whole yard of fryers or pullets would be sold off. I also remember them using an incubator, not their own, for hatching eggs and then large tray cages for the chicks that were the result. The incubator and chick cages were kept in the wash house, which was heated. Then the chicks were taken by someone, leaving behind enough for the Linas to restock their yards. They also raised white turkeys from chicks to full grown for the holiday market.

Troy:

In December of 2006, Carola's mother died and we all had funeral duties in Saint Charles, Missouri. There was a block of time available with nothing pressing to do. I suggested that we find the Great-great-grandparents Lina place, which wasn't too far away from the hotel. I took Maggie, Marykate, Shannon, Kirsten, and I'm not

The Linas in Troy Missouri

sure if anyone else came along. We drove out US61 and drove through the town.

There are vestiges of what I remember such as the old Sacred Heart Church, which is now a community center, the old Trojan Theater, which is still identifiable but not used as a movie house anymore, the Lincoln County Courthouse, Boone Street and the house where Grandma spent the last few years of her life, and the intersection of Highway J as it goes to Wright City.

We drove out that-a-way and found the old RR right of way, and there it was—the old house, now covered in a light green aluminum siding and still sitting there on the side of the road as it always had. The occupant was an older woman who had lived there for about four years. I explained what I was all about and she answered my questions as best she could. It was much smaller than I remembered. We'd been there once before, in the late sixties, when I took the kids to see it.

The Linas in Troy Missouri

2006

The Place

In 1932, it was four and a half acres located about two miles from the hardtop road and near the South Troy railroad station. It was along a Farm to Market road which was paved but with a clay and chert mixture that was dusty during the dry weather and stable but muddy during wet. The

The Linas in Troy Missouri

cars and wagons would follow the same path time after time and eventually there were two paths of fairly smooth road down more or less the middle. The road wended from farmhouse to farmhouse across the countryside from Troy to Wright City without regard for alignment except to get to within 100 feet, more or less, of each of the houses whenever possible.

As I recall, there were three houses leading up to the Linas' and two more leading away but there were more. The Bibbs' house, with a pond, was down the road, then the railway station, then another whose name I don't recall and further down Stevensons' place. There was also a creek we called Stevenson's Creek because it went through there. The two leading away were the Schmitts' and I don't remember the name of the other people but they were nice enough. Never saw the Bibbs or the others leading up to the Linas'.

I remember us waving to passing cars and realize now that there were so few passing cars that the event caused some excitement. There also was a

The Linas in Troy Missouri

horse drawn wagon going by from time to time as the driver went to Troy for supplies or whatever. And this would have been in the late forties. Rural electrification must have come during the late thirties and I wouldn't doubt that they lived without electricity for some time.

The isolation of the place makes me wonder if they were sold a bill of goods; if they bought a pig in a poke; or if their situation, real or imagined, was that desperate. Adding to my suspicions was their general demeanor and the lack of maintenance. It didn't make a conscious impression on me during those times but reflection now makes me wonder if it either wasn't their place, or if they were so disheartened by what they'd gotten themselves into that they just lived there as best they could.

They didn't have a car; that means they depended on the occasional neighbor going by to go into Troy or had supplies delivered to them by the stores in town. I only remember a small Kroger store but there were other stores supplying the necessaries for farm families in the area. In about

The Linas in Troy Missouri

the year 1950, Grandpa got a job as a liquor store clerk in Troy and rode a bicycle or took a cab to town; they never had a car.

The chicken feed may be the clue; they had to have it delivered because I remember it was in large cotton cloth sacks. An aside; the cotton sacking was a print material and Grandma would make shirts for us out of it. I had several even into my early teens. It could be that the chicken and egg collection man made notes of what was needed and either filled the order or had the supplies sent out to the place.

So there they were in 1932, no electricity, no car, no phone, only distant neighbors, and no kids. My dad was the last one at home in Walnut Park and they moved away from him. To hear him tell it, it was their way of telling him to make it on his own. I am getting a clue as to just how desperate their situation was. They must have used their last little bit of money to get this thing going and never again had enough to do anymore than scrape by.

The Linas in Troy Missouri

The Family

The following picture is of the entire family in November of 1941 with the exception of Arthur Boy, it must have been too cold for him to come out.

Many weekends and holidays were spent at Troy for as many as I can remember.

(For some unknown reason it appears upside down and several attempts at orienting it correctly failed so—upside down it is.)

The Linas in Troy Missouri

The Linas in Troy Missouri

The House

I could make a drawing of the house, and maybe I will, but I can describe it fairly accurately here. It started out as a rectangular house of one room down and one room up. It was about twelve feet by fifteen feet with a door in the front offset to the right side looking at it, a window to the left of the door, and a second window near the opposite end of that wall. On the far left were a rear exit door and a stairway that went to the upper room. The sink was on the rear wall, located there to access a cistern that collected rainwater which was delivered to the kitchen via a hand pump.

Sometime later, and before the Lina's moved in, a large addition, sans kitchen, was added to the first two rooms. It was accessed by a doorway on the right of the original room, which was the kitchen, as close as was practical to that end of the room.

This addition consisted of a dining room, parlor, two bedrooms and a sewing/utility room. The dining room was fairly large and, when electrification came, had a light in the center

The Linas in Troy Missouri

hanging over the table location. There was an archway to the adjacent parlor that was toward the road from the dining room and formed an el with the original rooms.

Off the parlor was a bedroom that likewise jutted toward the front, the other bedroom was off the dining room, and then the small sewing utility room off of that bedroom at the back of the house. There was a dirt cellar under this sewing room that housed preserves and this is also the room where there was an ice box. Around the house, from the kitchen door, along the side and across the front to the front bedroom, was a screened in porch.

There was a concrete pad outside the back of the dining room door. It was on this pad that a wash tub would become a bathtub in summer. We'd take a bath once in a while; at least every week but sometimes more frequently depending on what was going on. There was a lot of dust in August because it was so dry.

The Linas in Troy Missouri

Every Day Life

There isn't a lot that can be said about living day in and day out at the place. There are only a few snippets that I recall. First of all, I have to guess that they weren't as socially isolated as one might think. They belonged to Sacred Heart Catholic Church in Troy and I recall going to a picnic or two on the church grounds. This would indicate that they had a circle of friends who gave them support.

The fact that they were out in the country and still had their trips to town, either for church or to shop, would lead one to believe that they had neighbors upon whom they could rely. Then there's the fact that I played little league baseball when I was out there during the summer because the Schmitts' boys were on the Troy team and they were nice enough to include me. I was on the team and played in games against other towns on the diamond at the fairground or away.

The conclusion is that they had a rather complete life even though they lived outside of town. I

The Linas in Troy Missouri

think it probably improved as time progressed. In other words, it was quite miserable and lonely at first but over the years it improved as they got to know people and people got to know them.

A man who retired to Matthews County in Virginia asked me how many people I knew or who knew me in the shipyard. Then he posited there must be thousands; he said the population of the county was 5,000 and they all knew him within a few weeks of him and his wife moving into their place. That is probably how it was in Troy for the Linas.

Telephone

Sometime in the late forties telephone service was extended to the area. They had a big wooden box of a phone on the wall; it had a crank that operated a bell and a distinct ring that was theirs. All others on the party-line had distinct rings, in that way one knew when the call was for him. There was the nuisance of people listening in but then I remember Grandma doing it to others. That

The Linas in Troy Missouri

was their service all the time and it may have been upgraded to dial tone at some point.

Out Buildings

Along with the house on the property were several outbuildings. The "wash house" was a major and well-used building that sat close to the house just outside the door at the rear of the kitchen. It was about one step from one door to the other. That building was used as would have been a basement. It contained the laundry and storage. It was also used from time to time for incubating eggs and storing the newly hatched chicks. We would apply sulfur to our bodies in that room before going for walks in the fields as a preventative to ticks and chiggers. A large tree nearly blocked access to the back of the house from between the wash house and house but was a valuable provider of shade during the summer.

Behind the house and just outside the utility room was a pump house. There was a deep well that was the water supply for the place. It had a hand pump until about 1950 when Uncle John installed

The Linas in Troy Missouri

an electric motor powered pump. That was just the same time that I had grown big enough and strong enough to work the hand pump; this was a manly task in my mind and I was proud to be able to do it.

Alongside the wash house there was a driveway that consisted of two paths an axle width apart that ran from the road to the barn way up in the back of the place. As one walked this drive from the road, the fryer shed was on the left and further back than the wash house. It was a smallish shed with a chicken wire fence around a yard area. The mesh was supported by poles that were not in the ground; it was a loose fence that could be adjusted for size depending on how many chickens there were. This was also the turkey shed when required.

The next shed, and still on the left, was a wood shed, although I don't remember it containing any wood. It had the axe and double handled saw for splitting and cutting logs for the stove. There was also a load of soft coal dumped nearby each year

The Linas in Troy Missouri

for the winter and another load, which was an oddity.

There was a shoe factory in the town of Troy where heels were made for women's shoes. The vagaries of wood are such that there were always a certain percentage of rejects. Grandpa somehow arranged to buy these and had them delivered to the place by the truck load. They were used like any other wood for the kitchen stove.

Next down the drive and on the right was a large tool shed, it was more of a farm building than a shed and it had in it all the farm implements, mostly small tools such as shovels, rakes, potato rakes, hoes, a hand powered plow. This is where the rabbit hutches were located when he raised them for a while during WWII.

That was a common practice at the time. My dad built hutches on the smoke house at Oriole Avenue for the same purpose and got into the rabbit business for a while. We had rabbit for meals often and it seems every Sunday for a long

The Linas in Troy Missouri

time. We had it baked, fried, in stew, and even smoked. He would stretch the hides and I'd go with him to the fur processor when he sold them.

Next on our little walk there was the privy on the right that straddled a small drainage run behind the farm building. It was not very large but had two seats, a white one and a black. It was simply constructed with stud walls, board siding, and a sloping roof. The seats were directly over the little ditch and open to the air; quite exhilarating in winter. Grandpa solved the draftiness problem by tacking Life Magazines, a weekly photo publication at the time, to the studs. They served two purposes; they insulated as well as entertained while sitting. As I think back on this arrangement, it wasn't very sanitary.

Then on the other side of the privy rut were a potato field and then two more yards that were a coop and a barn. I was introduced to potatoes in this field. Grandma gave me a potato rake, showed me how, and then set me to work to dig out the potatoes. It was quite a revelation to me to see these clods turn out to be edible potatoes.

The Linas in Troy Missouri

The barn was big, in my mind, but small by any other standard. The coop is where the pullets were kept. There were always fewer of them than fryers or hens but the coop clean out was just as onerous as the roost for the hens. It was these roosts, the coop and barn, that Grandma had me clean out one summer and I never experienced anything quite like that again. I could hardly breathe, the smell was terrible.

There was no grass in the barnyard because of the chickens. I suppose they ate everything they could. There was always a rooster or two, but two usually resolved down to one after a while. The nests were in the barn and we'd collect eggs every day. It didn't take long to amass the two to four crates that were collected by the egg-man.

Some of the hens became possessive of their nests, these were called clucks, and had to be pushed off to get to the eggs. When pushed aside they would cluck, hence the name. If they were too much of a nuisance they became the base of a good chicken soup.

The Linas in Troy Missouri

The next and last item on the walk would have been the gate. It was the end of the property and opened into a field. There was no path but if you crossed that field you'd end up at the Schmitt's place. On either side of the gate were raspberry bushes that yielded enough every summer to eat fresh and make jam.

The rest of the property was open for cultivation but the ground wasn't very good. The field to the left of the drive on up to the road, which took a right angle turn at the property line and continued along the upper side, was almost always barren, just full of weeds. I recall grandpa pushing that hand powered plow but I don't think it yielded anything, ever.

On the other side of the house there was likewise a field. It was barren as well; I don't think I remember ever seeing anything but weeds in it. One day grandpa saw a wild rabbit in it, took his 22 caliber rifle, the one that my son John now has, and plinked it with a single shot, right in the head; thus to rodents and varmints.

The Linas in Troy Missouri

Between and behind the house, pump house and tool building was a garden plot where grandma grew a few herbs and vegetables. She was quite creative as a cook and home crafts person; by home crafts I mean sewing, knitting, and crocheting. Her chicken soup was memorable and I think she got a lot of the flavoring for it from this little garden.

Bobby

My cousin Bobby is/was about ten years older than I. He died several years ago after a long bout with tongue and mouth cancer. When he was a teenager we would spend summers together at Troy. I idolized him because he seemed to know so much and was able to think up a lot of things to do. We walked along Stevenson's Creek to find crawfish; he had little firecrackers and would blow them up. We marveled at how the shells turned red. This is a picture of the two of us, taken from behind as we walked across a bridge with our fishing poles. It sort of tells the story of Bobby and me.

The Linas in Troy Missouri

Bobby and Me

Bobby was Uncle Tony's son by his first wife, Olga. She died in childbirth when a second son, Arthur-boy, was born. This may have had a profound effect on Bobby who would have been about five

The Linas in Troy Missouri

or six when this happened. Except for Troy, I didn't see much of Bobby except when we visited Tony and Marion. They lived in several places around Saint Louis, rented a house at one point over in Walnut Park. When we went to see it, Bobby said there was a swimming pool in the basement. It really impressed me and I wanted to see it. He took me down and showed me a little puddle in the middle of the floor. Everyone had a good laugh about that.

Arthur-boy

Arthur was brain damaged at birth; his mother Olga died on the birthing table. Tony couldn't take care of him, work, and take care of Bobby, so Grandma Lina took Arthur-boy. I remember him sitting in a sling back lawn chair, all sort of curled up, looking around, unable to raise his head but turning it from side to side. It seemed like he was always ready to smile. He made little sounds but couldn't say anything.

He had to be fed baby food because he couldn't eat. And that's how it went for a long time until

The Linas in Troy Missouri

one day when I was about ten, I came down to breakfast at home and my dad said, "Arthur-boy died." He said more but that's what I remember. I cried, as I sat there, I don't know why I cried but cry I did.

The Browns

At some point, the Browns built a three room house across the road from the Linas' on land between the road and the railroad. It was of very low cost construction, frame, no foundation other than pads with cinderblock to the floor framing, asbestos siding, and without ornamentation of any kind. The driveway was from the front of the house to the road and simply two dirt tracks.

Mrs. Brown was an unfortunate soul. She was somewhat emaciated, several teeth missing, scraggily grey-black hair knotted to the top of her head with wisps going off in all directions. I have no idea how old she was but I'll bet she was much younger than she looked. She was, however, a kindly sort of person and often came over to talk to Grandma. She made a path through the scrub

The Linas in Troy Missouri

trees and bushes that were on the road right-of-way; that way she could take a short cut to Grandma's house. Her constant emphatic statement was, "Woman, I'm tellin' ya..."

She had at least two boys: George Washington and Thomas Jefferson, and at least one girl whose name I don't recall. All of them had holes in their teeth from cavities; I didn't know at the time what they were. Her husband was addicted to chewing tobacco to the extent that he slept with a wad in his cheek and a can near the bed for spitting.

I heard later that Tommy did well for himself but I don't know what happened to the rest of the family and I'm not really sure about Tommy; it's just an impression I have.

Rex

Uncle Andy came to my mom and dad's house with a little puppy that he got somewhere along the line. It was cute little fur ball, stumbling around barely able to walk. A decision was made to offer it to the Linas and when they saw it the

The Linas in Troy Missouri

next Sunday in Troy, they decided to keep it; I'm sure saying, what the heck, it may be fun.

The little puppy was diapered because he wasn't house trained and let loose wherever he was. Everyone enjoyed the little guy who seemed to have lots of personality. As he grew and matured into a dog, that was proven out over and over again.

Rex was my dog when I was there. He was protective and with me constantly. When some of us went on walks he would range out about a hundred yards and clear the way of anything that moved. Then there was the time that my mom was about to smack me and Rex growled at her. That was a punishable offense and he was reminded who was the boss.

One day he was with us as my dad and I were walking along Stevenson's Creek. He saw some cattle in the field and charged out after them to clear them out of our way. As he approached them, they formed a semi-circle with their heads down towards him in a formation. He stopped,

The Linas in Troy Missouri

sat a moment, cocked his head and went running around to the side in a flanking maneuver and broke their formation, scattering them in the field. It was quite remarkable.

He was the farm dog for the place. He would regularly, but not on any schedule like daily, go up to the hen yard and catch a chicken in his mouth, take it over to Bibbs' pond and take it in the water with him, swim out to the middle and let it go. The chicken would somehow get back to the edge of the pond and make its way back to the hen yard. Rex would swim back and wait until he was right next to me to shake the water off then roll in the dusty road. He was quite the clown!

Another day the Schmitts' dog, Shep, came waltzing by and Rex went after him. They were a jumble of fur and fangs for a while. Shep clamped down on Rex's manliness and there was quite a howl. The dogs separated and Shep went running away as fast as he could and never came back to our place again.

The Linas in Troy Missouri

Rex was the protector of the place and was well taken care of by Grandpa and Grandma. Then, just a few days after Grandpa Lina died; he took off down the road and was never seen again.

Cleo

Coming home from Holy Cross Church one Sunday morning I heard what I now know as bleating coming from the tall weeds on a vacant lot at the corner of Switzer and Gilmore. When I went and looked I saw a little goat tied by a rope to a stake. I fell in love with that little face.

Going on home, I asked my mom if I could have it. Why she said yes, only she knows. I took my money; it was $1.50, to the Uette's and asked about the goat. The son came out and I said I wanted to buy the goat. He asked how much money I had, I told him, he said to keep the fifty cents and to give him the dollar. I did and took the goat home.

We named her, Cleo. I lavished a lot of attention on her that day for a couple of hours, then went

The Linas in Troy Missouri

into the house.   My parents were busy redecorating the bedroom to make it the living room; refinished floors, textured walls, new paint on walls and ceiling. I was watching them work when I heard a knocking on the window. Cleo had pulled out her stake and was up on the porch, standing on her hind legs and knocking on the glass window with her front hoof. She was already spoiled.

She caused my dad a lot of trouble but I loved her. He built a stage for her in the one shed where she would be above any mess on the floor. I suppose he had to clean out the messes she made. She was always getting away, visiting the neighbors. We got calls, come get Cleo she's in my yard.

The crowning event unfolded one afternoon as my dad came home from the shop. He saw her eating the bark off of some sapling fruit trees he'd planted. Well he went ballistic, called her some bad names and went for her. She avoided him by going in a circle around him and just when he was about to unload on her with his hand, she pulled the rope tight and down he went. Oh, was he

The Linas in Troy Missouri

mad. The next Sunday we went to Troy with Cleo in the car. She was "given" to Grandma and then after a few months she found her way to a different farmer who had goats.

The Station

In 1984, Mom, Dad, Barb, Joe, Carola, and I went on a trip to the "old Country." Barb and I saw the railroad station in Bela Crkva and were both aware of the similarity of scene with the station at South Troy even without saying anything to each other about it at the time.

As one came around the bend in the road and down the gradual slope, one could see the South Troy Station just over on the left. There was a cinder paved parking area around it from the road to a short distance behind it and down-track.

The station was a frame building. It had a central office area with a bay window protruding toward the track for an agent, if there ever was one. On one side, and nearer the road was a waiting room with benches. The archway between the office

The Linas in Troy Missouri

and waiting room contained a large pot bellied stove in its center. A steel, heavy gage wire fence-type material formed a security barrier around the stove and to the arch on either side and above it. The other side and equally as large was a storage space for freight. Thus the building was symmetrical around the office.

The office contained a large wind up wall clock. Mr. Bobeen must have kept it wound, he was a man from town who received freight and shipped whatever was outbound. He was missing all but his index finger and thumb on one hand. He said it got caught in a corn husker. He came by occasionally, about once a week to do his thing. The office was so quiet when no one was around that the sound of the ticking clock filled the silence.

It was here that Tommy Brown hauled out a cigar box containing cigarette butts and offered one to me. I may have been ten or eleven at the time. I had experimented with cigarettes in grade school and I thought I knew what I was doing. He said, no— you inhale it, watch. I did and I thought I

The Linas in Troy Missouri

was going to die on the spot. That was the beginning of a long bout with tobacco that lasted until August of 1984 when I quit for the last time.

The Communists

Late in 1951, the Linas received a letter and photographs from Anton's sister Katrina and her family in Belgrade. There were pictures of his sister, her husband, her family, a son and his wife and their son. This caused quite a stir around the Sunday dinner table in Troy. The discussion was whether or not to reply to this letter. One can only be in awe of the communist phobia that existed during those years. It was during the McCarthy Hearings and everyone was very sensitive to having anything to do with anything communist.

The consensus reached at the time was to not reply to this letter and to my knowledge they never did. It is, in hindsight, a very troubling affair to think that something such as the witch-hunts that were going on that time could reach into the lives of humble people like the Linas and their

The Linas in Troy Missouri

sons. It is even more troubling to think that Anton's sister made this overture to him and was ignored.

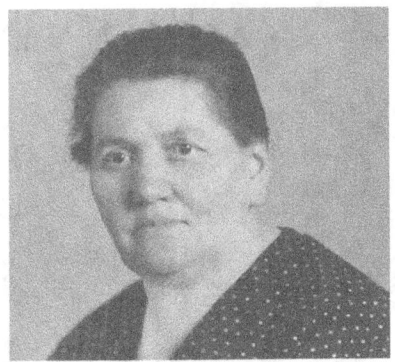

Aunt Kate, Grandpa's Sister

Aunt Kate's Husband

The Linas in Troy Missouri

Aunt Kate and Children

The Linas in Troy Missouri

How the Story Ends:

On Wednesday of the week I went to Boy Scout camp in the summer of 1952, I was surprised to see my dad's truck come to our campsite. He came to fetch me; Grandpa Lina died. He was laid out at McCoy Funeral Home in Troy, there was a Funeral Mass at Sacred Heart Church, and the body was brought to Calvary Cemetery in Saint Louis for burial.

Shortly thereafter there was an estate sale at the place in Troy. These affairs are as much a social as commercial event. People come from all around to see what the folks had and then to bid on it if they wanted it. It was a sort of revelation of the deceased family and a sale. Part of the price paid by the seller is to bare one's possessions to the assembly and part of the value received is to either gloat over or envy the family breaking up. The proceeds of this sale were given to Grandma and she moved into town. There she lived on Boone Street as a companion to an even older woman whose name I don't know.

The Linas in Troy Missouri

A few years later in 1956, she complained of chest pains while shopping in a department store in Saint Charles and died of a heart attack either there or shortly thereafter. There was likewise a Funeral Mass at Sacred Heart and the cortege took her body to Calvary Cemetery as well. It rained as we came out of the church and I recall Aunt Marion saying, "The angels are crying for Mom."

Epilog

When I took Theresa and Johnny to see the place in the late sixties, the woman living there showed me inside and out. It was recognizable, the sheds were down but the barn had been painted white. A lot of the trees and bushes were gone and the property had been diminished by the straightening of Highway J. The railroad station was gone as were the tracks. The loop around the station and Bibb's farm was lopped off by the straightening and there were two dead end vestiges of the old road servicing one side and the other of the railroad right-of-way.

The Linas in Troy Missouri

She said there had been other people who came by to see the place. I was puzzled because I didn't know what she was talking about. She tried to tell me who it was but I still couldn't understand. When I got home and talked to my mom about it she explained who it could have been.

It seems that Grandma Lina took in two foster boys at some point along the line; before Arthur-boy. She provided care to them for several years and they went on their way in the world. It was probably one, or both of these boys, who stopped by Troy to see the old place. This is a way of saying that with all that I remember, there's still a lot more that I don't know about the whole situation.